Made in the USA
Monee, IL
15 March 2021

62828868R00056